THE TROSSACHS

by
David Warnock

'The rocky summits, split and rent, formed turret, dome or battlement'

Sir Walter Scott

Callander. . . .

*the start of the tour, gateway to the Highlands
and a popular tourist centre.*

The tall spire of St Kessogs reaches into the blue skies above Ancaster Square. The square provides a focal point for many events—the pipe band plays on a summer evening.

Callander Meadows . . . .

where two lesser rivers meet to form the Teith. Also a home for the ever hungry mallard ducks.

Callander's television image, Tannochbrae is symbolised by Arden House, the home of Dr Finlay and his casebook.

Walk up to the Bracklinn Falls through the beautifully wooded Crags and take in Arden House on the way.

The Keltie Water pours over the giant rock steps of the falls into a deep gorge, fifty feet below the bridge.

Water coloured by the mineral chalybeate gives the Red Well its name. The water was taken by many to restore health and vigour.

The same water feeds a rich variety of plants and insects. In mid-summer there are flowers in every peaty hollow, here the marsh thistle feeds the pearl bordered fritillary.

The woodland mosaic of the Crags.

*The Scots pine, the tree of the Caledonian
forest and favourite haunt of the red squirrel.*

Winter sun striking the Jubilee Cairn, a viewpoint at the summit of Callander Crags.

Look north to the foot of Stuc a Chroin, a red deer stag in search of food brought to the low ground by winter snows.

Stroll out towards Kilmahog by the Teith and back to Callander along a leafy path. Leny House rests amidst its rich parkland.

Traditional craft skills are demonstrated at local woollen mills with plenty of tartans, tweeds and knitwear to choose from.

Waterfall and Wood . . . .

The Pass of Leny, where the river forces its way between the ancient highland rocks to join the more peaceful waters of the Teith.

Wild hyacinths in spring woodland shade. Strengthening sun encourages new life and new leaf.

The bold mass of Ben Ledi (hill of the gods) is a dominant feature in the Trossachs landscape. Although not a high mountain it attracts walkers, photographers and those who are simply admirers.

Westwards out along Loch Venachar . . . .

**Emptied by the Eas Gobhain and sheltered
between the Menteith Hills and Ben Ledi.**

By still waters . . . .

Ben Venue mirrored in Loch Achray providing tranquility for all. A mute swan glides past unruffled.

Almost on the shore of Loch Achray—the simple peace of the Trossachs Kirk.

Ben An rises above the autumn-tinted wood and quiet loch.

The heart of the Trossachs—Loch Katrine. Sir Walter Scott brought early fame to the dramatic scenery of the loch through his writings. Today the steamer named after him gives visitors the opportunity to slowly absorb the atmosphere.

Mountain, island, wood and loch.

Loch Katrine now forms a major part of Glasgow's water supply. The service road around the loch is open to everyone for walking and cycling . . . .

. . . . perhaps to see or hear a different kind of piper. The common sandpiper, a summer visitor to the loch shores.

A superb viewpoint and picnic area at the
David Marshall Lodge visitor centre above
Aberfoyle.

On, over the Duke's Pass where the Queen
Elizabeth Forest Park mixes trails, drives
and cycleways in a working forest. Many of
the trees are now maturing after forty to sixty
years of growth and the timber is ready for
use.

Roe deer favour the forest and graze in open areas at dawn and dusk.

A song thrush perches on a spruce branch at the woodland edge.

*Down into Aberfoyle, a busy town: west to
Loch Lomond, east to Stirling, south to
Glasgow and north to the Highlands.*

*Heading out along Loch Ard to distant Ben
Lomond.*

*Sunset from Ben An, gold on the silver of
Loch Katrine.*

About the author . . . .

David Warnock lives in Callander and works as a countryside ranger. With an understanding of his native land he is a perceptive landscape and wildlife photographer. In this album he demonstrates these skills by producing some beautiful and original photographs. An extensive traveller, David also enjoys hill walking and is a member of the local mountain rescue team.